STERLING'S GOLD

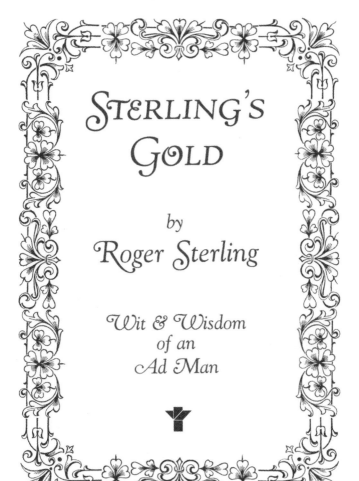

STERLING'S GOLD

by
Roger Sterling

Wit & Wisdom
of an
Ad Man

Published simultaneously in Canada
Printed in the United States of America

ISBN 978-0-8021-1989-6

Design by Charles Rue Woods and Matthew Enderlin

Grove Press
an imprint of Grove/Atlantic, Inc.
841 Broadway
New York, NY 10003

Distributed by Publishers Group West
www.groveatlantic.com

10 11 12 13 14   10 9 8 7 6 5 4 3 2 1

Table of Contents

Gentle Reader,

After devoting most of my life to the
nefarious trade known as advertising,
I thought it was time to share some of
the pearls that I've been fortunate enough
to accumulate. Now keep in mind that
oysters don't open easy and every one of
those gaudy baubles started off as a grain
of sand.

As you may find out, I'm not a writer.
On some level, that's a point of pride
because it steered me away from the cliché
of autobiography. I had no desire to waste
your and my time trying to turn a list of
events into a campaign of triumph.

So here it is . . . a few things over-
heard, a few things to live by, and hell,
a few things I've apparently said and had
repeated to me the morning after a party
when I called to make amends. As I said,
advertising's been half my life and I'm
probably off by 50 percent. But dammit,
if it hasn't felt like fifteen minutes.

You'll see the dedication reads differently, but I'd like to thank and apologize in advance to the following entities:

1. Shakespeare.

2. Lincoln. The President and the Continental.

3. That nameless genius that first put a pickled onion in a glass of vodka.

4. People who can really write. I'm sorry my book got published first.

5. J. Press., Brooks Brothers, and Renaldo, my tailor with the golden needle.

6. Hotel rooms where the bed is always the center of attention.

7. Arpege, Shalimar, Joy, Chanel No. 5. It's all your fault.

8. Redheads.

9. Wives.

10. New York City, the cradle of civilization.

I should also probably thank my agent, Ira, for almost believing in me, and the folks at Grove Press who urge you to buy ten. They make great coasters.

Sincerely,

Roger Sterling

Roger Sterling

Dedicated to the men who still wear hats
and the women that love them.

*On
Advertising*

What else is there?

When you run an ad that is positive, you're only convincing the people who are already voting for you. But when you run an ad that's critical, you get a shot at the people on the fence.

♦ ♦ ♦

When a man
gets to a point
in his life
when his name's
on the building,
he can get
an unnatural
sense of
entitlement.

♦ ♦ ♦

Dogs are winners.

I'LL TELL YOU WHAT

BRILLIANCE IN ADVERTISING IS:

NINETY-NINE CENTS.

SOMEBODY THOUGHT OF THAT.

I don't know if anyone ever told you that half the time this business comes down to: "I don't like that guy."

On Clients

My dad used to say,
"This is the greatest job in
the world except for one thing —
the clients."

Clients like the thrill
of young talent.

Don't you love the chase?
Sometimes it doesn't work out.
Those are the stakes.
But when it does work out —
it's like having that first cigarette.
Your head gets all dizzy,
your heart pounds,
your knees go weak.
Remember that?
Old business is just old business.

THE ONES WITH THE
BEST PRODUCTS
MAKE THE WORST CLIENTS.

I don't think it's a bad idea
to have a chance
to out-drink our clientele.

If Lee Garner, Jr. wants

three wise men flown in from

Jerusalem, he gets it.

I love how they sit
there like a couple of
choir boys but you know
one of them's leaving
New York with VD.

You know what my father used to say? Being with a client is like being in a marriage. Sometimes you get into it for the wrong reasons and eventually they hit you in the face.

IT PROBABLY DIDN'T HELP THINGS THAT OUR BILLINGS CREPT UP FOR NO APPARENT REASON. EVENTUALLY AN ACCOUNTANT IS GOING TO READ THE MAIL.

The day you sign a client is the day you start losing them.

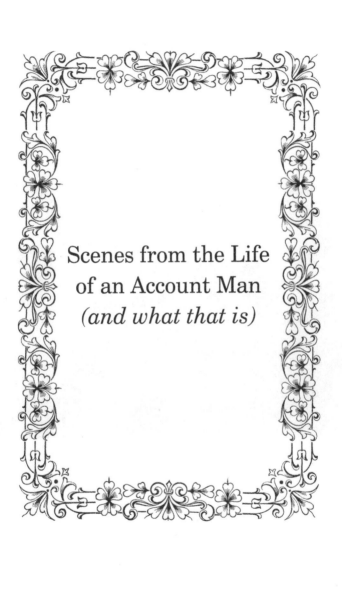

Scenes from the Life
of an Account Man
(and what that is)

THEY DON'T SEEM TO GIVE AWARDS FOR WHAT I DO.

You know no one
who's ever been
associated with an
actual event has
thought it's been
portrayed honestly
in the newspaper.

I'm not going to sit here and brag about how big I am.

*It's about
listening to people
and never saying
what's really on
your mind.*

I'm being punished
for making my job look easy.

YOU DON'T VALUE WHAT I DO
ANYMORE THAN THEY DO.
YOU'RE NOT GOOD
AT RELATIONSHIPS BECAUSE
YOU DON'T VALUE THEM.

*Things to Say
to Creatives*

*I'm going to count to three
and then I'm going to start saying
a lot of words you don't like,
sweetheart.*

Oh, good.
I got you when you're
vulnerable.

I don't know if you were drunk
or not drunk,
but that was inspired.

I never get used to
the fact that most of
the time it looks like
you're doing nothing.

LOOK AT THIS PLACE.
I DON'T WANT TO SOUND
SENTIMENTAL BUT IT'S
NOT JUST ACCOUNTS.
LOOK AROUND HERE
AT WHAT YOU HAVE.

I've worked with a lot of men like you, and if you had to choose a place to die, it would be in the middle of a pitch.

*Errol Flynn is gone
and so is my taste
for swordplay.
You two need to
put them away.*

If I was worried,

I'd ask you what you've got.

But I'm not.

So I'm just going to assume

that you've got something.

Which means *you*

should be worried.

The problem is
I don't know
if you don't
want to do this
here or you
don't want
to do this at all.

♦ ♦ ♦ ♦ ♦

I'LL PAINT YOU THE
PICTURE THAT I HAVE
IN MY MIND
BUT IF IT'S TRUE,
I MIGHT KILL MYSELF.

Let's not get
emotional here.
There's no reason we
can't talk this out.

Your kind, with your gloomy
thoughts? And your worries.
You're all busy licking
some imaginary wound.

I want to see
what you look like
with your tail
between your legs.

*Big talent
attracts
big clients.*

Hope we're not
interrupting
this crisp and
engaging portrait
you're painting.

*YOU WIN A FEW TIMES,
YOU GOTTA START REALLY
PUTTING IT OUT THERE.
YOU KEPT BETTING
THE SAME THING.*

♦ ♦ ♦

I'VE LOST MEN LIKE YOU BEFORE.

IT USUALLY HAD TO DO WITH MY

UNEXPRESSED CONFIDENCE.

I THINK YOU'RE ONE IN A MILLION.

♦ ♦ ♦

Grunt once for yes.

On the Art
of Seduction ...

It's Labor Day weekend.
Between now and Monday
we have to fall in love
a dozen times.

Reservation at home. I've had those. Easiest ones to break. Besides, they love it when you keep them guessing. It adds spice.

See her this weekend.
You hit it off?
Come turkey day,
maybe you can stuff her.

REMEMBER,
WHEN GOD CLOSES A DOOR,
HE OPENS A DRESS.

...and what to say to close the deal

Have a drink.
It'll make me look younger.

I WAS JUST GIVING HER
A HARD TIME.
CAN I INTEREST YOU IN
THE SAME?

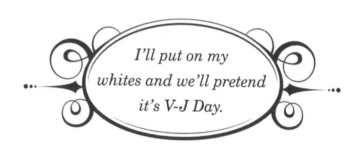

*I'll put on my
whites and we'll pretend
it's V-J Day.*

Don't make me use my spurs on you.

Where'd you get that sweater?
I want to make sure my daughter
never buys it.

I could tell I was rubbing you the wrong way so I thought, why not have someone rub you the right way?

On Drinking...

4:30?

Close enough.

♦ ♦ ♦

Ah, that's where
you've been.

You don't know how to drink.
Your whole generation.
You drink for the wrong reasons.
My generation?
We drink because it's good.
Because it feels better
than unbuttoning your collar.
Because we deserve it.
We drink because
it's what men do.

*T*hey say once you start drinking alone,
you're an alcoholic.
I'm really trying to avoid that.

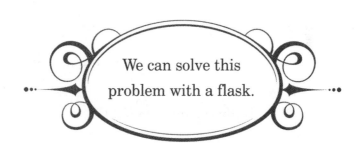

We can solve this
problem with a flask.

My podiatrist went to Hazelden. Came back a new man with great stories. Only drinks beer now.

*...and those who
no longer do*

There's all the
talk about drinking,
where they start
with the funny
stories and they
end up crying.

They're self so-righteous.
I never pissed *my* pants.
This guy killed a man
with a motorboat.
You know what gets you
over something like that?
Drinking.

I bet daily friendship
with that bottle
attracts more people
to advertising
than any salary you
could dream of.

Words to
Take Charge By,
and Other
Management
Insights

Now if the adults can weigh in?

*E*veryone thinks you're a fine fellow,
       but if I were you,
I'd go out there and make rain.

It looks like you're all
going to engage in a little
mid-level camaraderie,
so I'll be on my way.

So you're in here now,
I'm smiling,
what do you want?

I'm glad everybody can make it sound like they're working so hard.

I know that your generation
went to college instead of serving,
so I'll illuminate you.
This man is your commanding
officer. You live and die
in his shadow. Understood?

♦ ♦ ♦ ♦ ♦

Throw yourself on the grenade.
Protect the agency.
You're a partner now.

If we can switch to
a conversation about
paying clients . . .

All I'm saying is,
we should be going
after something as
big as what we had.

YOU PEOPLE ARE NOT

WATCHING ENOUGH

TELEVISION.

IT IS YOUR JOB.

THE SHOWS

AND THE ADS.

HONEY, I HAVE A SIX-THIRTY
DINNER RESERVATION.
UNLESS YOU WANT TO PULL
ME THERE IN A RICKSHAW,
I HAVE TO GET GOING.

*T*hey fired all the guys in the middle and moved up their mail room staff, right before all the salaries got expensive. Smart.

When all you have to do
is hold their hands,
jerk 'em off.
Is that so hard?

I told him to be himself.
That was pretty mean, I guess.

Don is talent.
You know how to deal
with that don't you?
Just assume that he
knows as much about
business as you do,
but inside there's
a child who likes
getting his way.

*I'd like to stay and get
all sentimental with you,
but I have to go
and give a Chinaman
a music lesson.*

Your loyalty
is starting to become
a liability.

WE NEED YOU TO CONTINUE
YOUR EXCELLENCE IN
ADVERTISING BUT ALSO TO
START TREATING THIS LIKE
PART OF A BIGGER BUSINESS,
WHICH IT IS.

♦ ♦ ♦

You might
have to
come in
and be an
advocate
for yourself.

♦ ♦ ♦

Fine. If you want to tuck it
between your legs, I'll call him.
But I have to warn you,
I'm going to drop your name.

No regrets fellas.

We were in it,

that's the important thing.

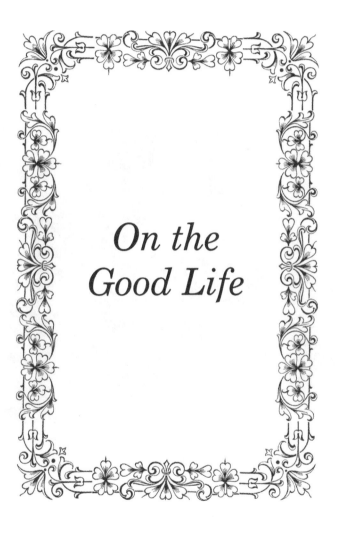

*On the
Good Life*

*One egg is good,
two eggs are better.*

I WOULD NEVER BUY
A SAILBOAT.
I DON'T WANT TO DO
THINGS MYSELF.
FOR THAT PRICE,
A BOAT SHOULD HAVE
A MOTOR.

My mother had a chinchilla.
I was always on the verge of a
romantic relationship with it.

Oysters Rockefeller,
Beef Wellington, Napoleons.
We leave this lunch alone
and it'll take over Europe.

♦ ♦ ♦ ♦ ♦

Do you know how invigorating it is to go in and write a check for sixty-five hundred dollars and not care? Secondly, not to get too deep before the cocktail hour, but do I need to remind you of the finite nature of life?

He was a bold man
that first ate an oyster.

Like the song says,
"Enjoy Yourself,
It's Later Than You Think."

YOU KNOW WHEN YOU
LEAVE YOUR SHOES OUTSIDE
THE DOOR HERE,
SOMEBODY POLISHES THEM.

*On Business
Ethics*

Plagiarism.
That's resourceful.

I TRY TO BE
AS CIVILIZED AS
YOU CAN BE.

SINCE WHEN IS
FORGIVENESS A BETTER QUALITY
THAN LOYALTY?

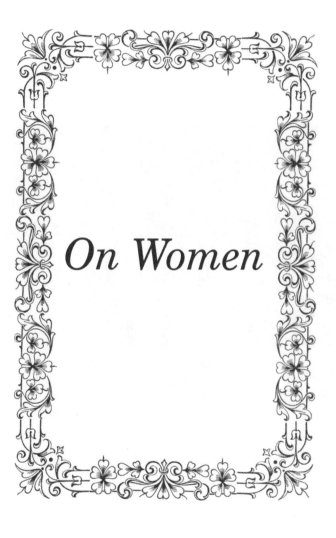

On Women

I am very comfortable with my mind.
Thoughts clean and unclean.
Loving — and the opposite of that.
But I am not a woman, and I think it
behooves any man to toss all female
troubles into the hands of a stranger.

♦ ♦ ♦ ♦ ♦

One night, years ago, I got very drunk.
I drive home to my building, pulled into
the garage and parked in my spot.
I get in the elevator, it's late, no operator,
I go up to the twelfth floor, get out.
I'm walking down the hall, it was pink
and orange, I remember how ugly it was.
Then suddenly, my key won't fit in the door —
it wasn't my building. I guess what
I'm saying is at some point we've all parked
in the wrong garage.

That glow of
pure youth. It's like they
hit thirty and somebody
puts out a light.

You know what they want? Everything. Especially if the other girls have it. Trust me, psychiatry is just this year's candy-pink stove.

I like redheads.
Their mouths are like
drops of strawberry jam
in a glass of milk.

On Love
and Marriage ...

I've been married for over twenty years,
I know the difference between a spat
and spending a month on the couch.
Don't go to bed angry.

If you put a penny in a jar
every time you make love
in the first year of marriage
and then you take a penny
out of the jar every time you
make love in the second year,
know what you have?
A jar full of pennies.

Desi and Lucy. Please.

He's divorcing her.   Again.

Did he wake up one morning and say,

"Oh yeah. I forgot. I hate you."

What makes a man marry

the same woman twice?

Mona had a dream once
where I hit the dog with the car.
She was mad at me all day,
and I never hit the dog.
We don't even have a dog.

Can somebody please get
my wife out of the kitchen?
I have something very
nice to say about her.
But while we're alone. . . .

People make mistakes.
You feel bad about it.
You think things over.
And in the end, you do
the grand gesture for her.

All I'm going to say is,
do you want to be right,
or do you want to be married?
I know marriage isn't
a natural state, but you do it.

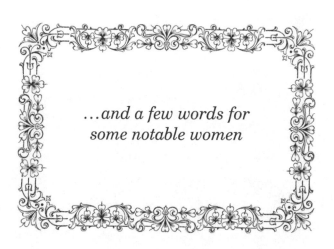

...and a few words for some notable women

Do you have any idea how unhappy
I was before I met you?
I was thinking of leaving my wife.

Look, I want to tell you something
because you're very dear to me.
And I hope you understand this
comes from the bottom of my
damaged, damaged heart.
You are the finest piece of ass
I ever had and I don't care
who knows it. I am so glad that
I got to roam those hillsides.

We were not in *Casablanca*.
The only similarities were that
you left me for another man.
That woman got on the plane
with a man who was going
to end World War II, not run
her father's dog food company.

But I guess you could keep it.

I mean, when he comes home, who's gonna

know the difference? Lots of GI's came home

to a little surprise. No one did the math.

It wouldn't be my child, let's make that clear.

I mean, if he comes home.

I've had a lot of time
to think about the
things I've done and
been sorry about.
And being with you is
not one of them.

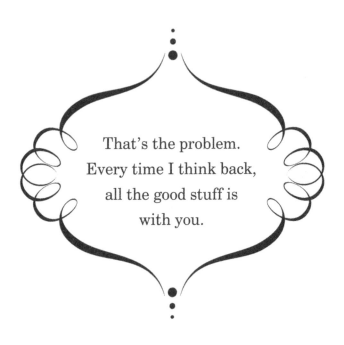

That's the problem.
Every time I think back,
all the good stuff is
with you.

*Things to Say
to Save the Deal*

*P*lease. Eat our sweet meats, drink our wine. I understand that one of our copywriters took a Yetta Wallenda size misstep.

♦ ♦ ♦

WE WILL SHAKE HEAVEN
AND EARTH, YOU KNOW THAT.
JUST TELL ME IT'S
FOR SHOW BEFOREHAND
BECAUSE I SWEAR,
YOU'RE GONNA KILL ME.

♦ ♦ ♦

*I shall be both
dog and pony.*

Let me put it in
account terms.
Are you aware of the
number of hand jobs
I'm going to have to give?

On Life

Enjoy it.
One minute you're drinking in a bar and
they come and tell you your
kid's been born, next thing you know —
they're heading off to college.

My father was the tallest, handsomest, vainest man in New York and he got his nails done. He had his fourth coronary behind the wheel and hit a tree. Windshield severed his arm and he was dead so they never put it back on. In the casket he had one hand, the nails were perfect.

White hair is distinguished
but the whiskers are a bit
Father Time.

ONCE YOU SAY THAT,

YOU'RE NOT DISCREET ANYMORE.

*M*aybe every generation thinks
the next one is the end of it all.
I bet there were people in the Bible
walking around, complaining about
"kids today."

My mother always said,
"Be careful what you wish for,
because you'll get it, and then
people will get jealous and
try to take it away from you."

*You want to be on
some people's minds.
Some people's
you don't.*

I always liked chocolate ice cream,
but my mother made us eat vanilla
because it didn't stain anything.

MY MOTHER WAS RIGHT.
IT'S A MISTAKE TO BE
CONSPICUOUSLY HAPPY.

♦ ♦ ♦ ♦ ♦

*All I was saying was
this is the office and that's life,
and this is good and that's life.*

*On Some Memorable
Colleagues*

FREDDY RUMSEN

The last time Freddy Rumsen
had a cup of coffee,
it was one of five being poured
down his throat by a cop.

DON DRAPER

An ad-man who doesn't
like to talk about himself.
I think I may cry.

PETE CAMPBELL

I can give you my assurance that
nothing good will happen to that boy,
though I can't seem to keep
my word on that, hard as I try.

IDA BLANKENSHIP

She died like she lived —
surrounded by the people
she answered phones for.

*A Final
Word*

♦ ♦ ♦

BELIEVE ME,

SOMEWHERE IN

THIS BUSINESS

THIS HAS

HAPPENED

BEFORE.

♦ ♦ ♦

Acknowledgments

The following people need to be acknowledged for their significant contributions to either making this book, or the character of myself, Roger Sterling, come to life.

Matthew Weiner
John Slattery
Scott Hornbacher
Keith Addis
Marcy Patterson
Janie Bryant
and
Linda Brettler

And of course all of the writers and directors that help feed me these lines.

And last but not least, my dear friend for over forty years, Amy Hundley, and her team at Grove/Atlantic.